Beyond The Guarded Walls Of My Soul

Stacey Raymond

Presentation by *BookLeaf Publishing*

Web: www.bookleafpub.com

E-mail: info@bookleafpub.com

ISBN: 9789357619684

First edition 2022

DEDICATION

This is for all of you who have gone through their own journeys. No journey is the same but we're all connected around the world. Where we feel less alone, knowing there are millions of compassionate, empathetic people. Even without knowing we would be there in a heartbeat through our troubling times. As well as love and support for everything we've achieved and survived through. You are worthy, you are loved, you're best just simply being you.

ACKNOWLEDGEMENT

I have to start by thanking Samuel. For all your support and inspiration, it was when you walked into my life that gave me the boost that all my dreams could become reality . Thank you so much you've truly touched my heart to the deepest realm of my soul.

PREFACE

Through domestic abuse in home and relationships. To where I found my calling to spiritual growth. That led me to my path to finding twin flame.

Perfectly Intertwined

Have you ever stopped to wonder about the extraordinary feeling love from the right person can bring? It makes you sing in the shower when you think no one's listening. The depth of connection you have to the one you're with. To know they will love you for truly being you. Be there to support you when you're up on top of the world. That is when you know their feelings are true. Even when you're down, they'll make you feel anything is achievable. Just have to believe in yourself as much as they do. They say the river runs deep, but how do they truly know? It's never been about water. It's the meaning of the deepest connection between two beings. How they flow so effortlessly through time. Like waves moving towards the shoreline. Perfectly together, perfectly intertwined.

Within The Universe

As the birds chirp when the morning rises.

Whether or not we have blue skies.

Deep as the ocean and far past our view.

Into the galaxy I only dreamed one day would come true.

To find the one where one day I would feel.

The feeling of true love I always wondered if it was real.

You came into my life right from my dreams.

Now I believe anything in life is possible, regardless of how crazy we think it seems.

You're everything I dreamt of, wished for and more.

You flung wide open my heart's door.

I finally found the one who had the key to my
soul.

Loved you before now and into forever more.
Between the moon and the stars, even though
there is distance, a part that connects them as
one within the universe. Being in your arms
feels like I'm wrapped in a beautiful galaxy
shining brightly.

May your day go smoothly. Like your smile
shines like the brightest star in the galaxy. Hot
like the sun and amazingly breathtaking just like
the moon. The only thing better within the
Universe is how many reasons why I know I
love you.

Love Within The Seasons

Even though the leaves change colours when fall
arrives. Nothing in the entire universe will
change my love for you. Every day our love
blossoms. It grows like flowers in between
spring and summer with the warmth in the air.
Our love is also like fall and winter with all the
amazingly beautiful colours. Our love forever
blossoms & grows. Just like all the seasons, it
has so many beautiful views and wonders to
behold. I see myself every day holding you until
we're grey and old. Most roses are red.
While all stems are green.
Regardless of the flower.
They're all beautiful and unique.
They warm your heart & make you smile.
That's the exact feeling I have when we're
together. Even though it feels like a small while.
I'll cherish every moment that we spend
together. I'll love you even more with every
passing day.

The Rising Of The Phenix
From The Ashes

Once shy and secluded, to not be seen or heard. You may think I had a horrific childhood. It's not completely absurd. It was only my adoptive mom that wore her angel mask in disguise. While all along behind closed doors I knew and felt it was a lie. From the constant belittling, rude remarks to the overall neglect. Sometimes I always wondered why what in the actual heck? Why did I deserve to be treated like an outcast? You were the one that chose me. Deep down inside, I knew there was more I had to see. Stuck in a negative spiral, I felt I was on my way to hell. Prayed and hoped someone would come along and cast a spell. Save me from the torture, save me from the pain. Day by day, I felt like I was going more and more insane. At least it was for a short while, as she felt we were too much of a burden to keep. That was my first glimpse of heaven when I landed at my adoption dad's feet. The only one who showed me what true unconditional love was supposed to be. Stuck in my subconscious mind at a very young age, I felt pure defeat. Unable to see what was real and what was full of deceit. All I knew I wanted to escape to avoid this being on repeat. I truly was lost not a soul to help while I felt bound by my feet. Trapped in such a treacherous soul. Didn't know which way to go. I often hide my face so others couldn't see the true pain. It didn't matter if the days were sunny, it felt like there was only rain. I'd fake a smile and nod to make it seem like I could understand. All the while, I knew my adoptive mom had the upper hand. Even though there were sporadic 2-day visits, I knew it was part of her plan. Not until I was an adult was I able to see she was in so much emotional pain. She was reflecting on what she'd been through right on to me. She wasn't doing it for gain. Most likely not being taught herself. That only inflicts more pain on others while it keeps you on a shelf. Even though I've been through some truly unspeakable things. I do forgive her not for herself, but more for me. Where there is no forgiveness to one's self, you cannot be set free. I had so much to learn in so many life lessons. Didn't know I would go through way worse. It constantly had me guessing. Is this the way life was permanently going to be? Or was there something more beautiful and amazing in store for me? Along the way, I did lose my faith and didn't know why it felt like I was cast into a world of hate. At least that's the way I felt until my mid thirties I finally started seeing my fate.

Right at perfect timing, I was starting to feel it maybe too late. Puzzle piece by puzzle piece, things started to fall in place. I started regaining my faith, I started to understand amazing grace. Never lose your faith nor lose your hope. There's so much more to life than just learning to cope. Once you see Devine's great plan. You'll reach the same realization I did and finally understand.

It's Not In Our Destiny To Stay Forever Apart

You are my mountain that meets my sea. It doesn't matter how hard the climb will be standing together, it will be a breeze. Once at the top, we can only go up from there. Then we'll see what we have with each other is far beyond compare. The majority of the time, we were always focused on why life was so unfair. Cherishing every moment but wanting to run in fear as little as the drop of a hair. Wanting to be together to share our love. Knowing we have been brought together by a higher power above. It's always the fear that makes us run scared. We just needed to have faith and know what's been prepared. Throughout our lives we've been taught many hurtful lessons about what we don't want in our lives. Not having faith and being stuck in fear will lead us to our very demise. Having faith and knowing what we have between us is destined to be. Place your hand in mine and know my heart is for you and yours is for me. What we have deep in our souls is where we know we can feel safe. A deeper feeling of home. You know deep down it's not too late. With forgiveness deep down in our hearts. We know this is only a separation for more growth, not a destiny apart. I love and miss you more than you let yourself know. Can't wait till the day you decide you feel safe to come home. We'll start the rest of our journey with a clean slate. As we know, holding onto past pain won't bring us a blissful fate. Till the day comes when we see each other again. I miss you and love you forever, my twin flame, my love, my partner, my best friend. Know you are safe within me and my love for you burns till the very end.

Warm Embrace

May our warm embrace get you through your day. With the chilly breeze in the air.

May the warmth in our kiss fire your soul. To keep you warm to the depths of your heart. Just before the coldness of the day starts to get to your core.

You'll be back in my warmth for us to keep sharing our love. Making and cherishing more memories of us in the many lifetimes ahead of us.

Music To My Soul

Like the birds waking us in the morning with their lovely melody. Your voice is like music to my soul. As the warmth of the sun warms our bodies.

Only your embrace warms my heart. Every day with you is a blessing with every passing moment. I keep these memories safe in my heart as I cherish every single one of them. You make my heart, soul, body and mind at peace surrounded by your love. I want to spend the rest of my days sharing my love and showing you how much I love you.

One Moment Too Long

I send you morning hugs and kisses to help guide you throughout your day. It won't be long before we're back by each other's side to share more memories in each and everyway. Each moment that passes without you is one moment too long, but knowing I have you forever is the tune of my heart's song.

All It Takes Is One

From just one moment

From just one kiss

From just one touch

Radiates our love through our mind, body and

soul.

A connection like this is far from the

imagination anyone can think of when they think

of what is true bliss. The power the slightest

thing has is far beyond any level of magnitude

for so many reasons and more why I Love You.

Never Ever

Never ever will I ever runaway. I know I am spiritually stronger. It's my destiny to stay .
Never ever should I have run away in fear, when all I ever wanted was to be by your side to keep you near.
Never ever should I ever have allowed negative thoughts and patterns to entrap me.
When I knew you were my twin flame, the love of my life, the best friend I could share everything with from the very depths within me. Never will I ever repeat this cycle of running in fear. I will only ever stay by your side, love you and always keep you near. Near to my mind, my heart, my body, my soul. For the rest of my life I am yours forever more.

Set The World On Fire

She set the world on fire as her cries rang out for anyone to save her. Is anyone listening as she cried to herself in the corner? After years of reaching out in her time of need. Cut off from family, friends and loved ones. No one heard, no one came. As much as she fought within herself to push forward. A deeper part just wanted to fade away. As she felt like she only mattered to others' needs, and what they could benefit from her. It always made her feel like she was worthless and no one would want her as she should be lucky. Just to have the one she was with her & she's not worthy of anyone else who would ever want such a slob as she gets told multiple times a day. Just look at you. Sometimes I wonder why I'm even with you. You count yourself lucky without me you'd be nothing. He would show her in very sporadic brief glimpses of hope to hang on. Some flowers here or there, even the slightest kiss, would give her hope things would change. Always making excuses why his anger makes him break things that are always said to be her fault. If it wasn't for her, he wouldn't be so angry all the time. Maybe things would change as she softly wiped the tears from her eyes. But sadly, it was just a facade to get her to stay, as he knew no one else would go through hell and back again for him. Breaks you down so you fall for the smallest of hope in a forever loophole in the demonic chaos. She always second guessed herself this cannot be love. If it was, why does it make me feel this way, she asked herself. But the fear had now been instilled deep in her mind as he broke her soul. That's all she'd ever be worth. To obey and do as you are told or fear my wrath when I unleash my power if you disobey me. Go ahead & leave with an evil laugh. You'll see we're all the same.

The Haunted Soul

She's haunted that she has to go to a place she doesn't want to be.

Filled with depression, this feeling will never leave.

Knowing what she's walking into, what the weekend has in store.

Having to walk through her adoptive mother's door.

A place where unconditional love truly doesn't exist.

She always questioned herself what did I do to deserve a life like this.

To be yelled at and belittled for every little thing.

All she ever wanted was a place that her heart could open and sing.

She had small glimpses of that of her past.

The unconditional love of her adoptive father

but she knew it would come to pass.

Not that her adoptive dad's love would change

as he loved her like his own.

But she struggled to believe once older if her

heart would ever have a home.

Because her adoptive mother made her believe

she was an outcast who would never fit in.

Trapped deep in her mind, always feeling stuck

within.

The Broken Soul Of A Twin Flame

Like the waves of the ocean crashing into the
shore.
It is like how my heart was shattered into a
million pieces on the floor.
Now when the sunrises into a new day.
It is just a constant remainder of your love you
took away.
Making me feel abandoned under the moonlight
and the stars.
It's completely unknown why you've stolen all
the pieces of my heart.
I truly felt our love was meant to be right from
the very start.
I apologize for all my trauma scars that made
this seem so impossibly hard.
Even though along the way things weren't
always bright and blue.
Deep within my soul I felt my dreams had
finally came true.
Finally, someone with such a vibrant intensity of
true passionate love.
To me, you felt like my home someone sent to
me from above.

Someone who made me feel that I love you was
felt deep inside.
Every part of you opened up every part of me
and made me feel alive.
Now that you've gone away, I feel lost and very
broken inside.
I still hear the birds but they sing a different
tune.
I think they feel the intensity of what I'm going
through.
All I had dreamt and envisioned of our future is
yet to come.
Once within our grasp, but feel a part of you,
decided to run.
Was it really for another or just running scared.
Having anxiety and fear, feeling very
unprepared.
You didn't have faith thinking we'd make it
together till we're old and grey.
Guess we'll both never know because you
decided not to stay.
You said you felt my spiritual growth and felt
things had changed.
Told me you were so much closer to me
everyday.
So, with all the unknowns, only one question
remains?
Why, oh why did you turn and walk away?

Will we reconcile and have a harmonious future
like we both envisioned so many times before?
That's left to the unknown if you should walk
back through my door.
As much that has been left to the unknown, I
understand why there maybe fear.
But one thing you should have felt deep inside is
my love will always be here.
The only one I've ever felt destined to be true.
Even with all we've been through, I feel and
mean every day I love you.
Regardless of what happens, I wish you the best.
You were the only one that brought down the
walls around my heart. I always know I felt
every last beat deep in my chest of how much I
love you. Above all, you have been the only one
I felt that truly loved me. Also, the only one that
made me feel like I could be authentically
myself and feel safe enough to be me.

In My Heart You'll Always Be

Every day as the minutes pass by. I'm feeling more optimistic you'll come back to stay and be mine.
You'll say that you're sorry it was all a horrible mistake.
Coming in quickly, as you fear, with each passing moment, you may be too late.
What we have isn't broken, it's clear to see.
I was sent to you and you were sent to me.
Through the universe, it's guided by archangels and divine time.
Know that we've truly started to heal our traumas no more rewinding.
Finally, living in each moment with each passing day.
We have so much catching up with so many words left to say.
Even unspoken, we know each other's truths.
I can finally see with all the clouds fading away so we can see through.
No one's loved me the same feeling you have about the way I love you.
We know this is destined to be. Our dreams have finally come true.

We have what it takes to see each other till the
end of time.
With your heart open to me the way you are in
mine.
There is one thing I have to say. I will love you
more and more with each passing day.
Deep in my heart and soul is where you're
destined to stay.
Not just for the present days that pass us by. I
know I'll be with you for the rest of my life.

Self-sabotagingly triggered

From all the past pain and horrific things throughout life I've been avoiding to feel. It is when I knew I needed to begin my journey and start to heal.

Back as far as I can remember, when I was a little one. I thought life as a child was supposed to be filled with fun.

Back then I didn't realize what was my actual fate. Crossing my fingers and praying, I hoped it was not too late.

Not realizing every moment was a lesson to learn. Always thinking when, oh when is it going to be my turn?

Not having much to look back on fondly of all the things I miss. It is hard to think of the moments for me to truly reminisce.

With so many forms and shapes of abuse. I was starting to feel like it's my fault why I always get used.

Being molested by my adoptive mother's boyfriend, then drugged and raped by my stepdaughter's dad. It's a very harsh understatement to say that with this I was feeling more than just a little mad.

Then just when I thought the cycle of abuse would end. My middle daughter's dad had a very much different plan.

After my stepdaughter's dad, I had knowledge of some of the lessons. So when I saw the same patterns and knew I had to leave, I wasn't left guessing.

We left when she was still tiny and small. Having to be a true mama bear, I put up my walls super tall.

These are just little tidbits here and there from my past abusive relationships I escaped. Remember anyone in the same circumstances? It's never too late.

I have been tossed through the ringer like so many of you. One that hasn't been through it wouldn't have the foggiest clue.

Of the trauma and scars you have to heal within. Without introspection and healing from the past.

Will only lead to self-sabotaging everything healthy in your journeys path. Without the shadow work, nothing in your present will last.

I know it hurts. I've been there too deep in the depths of emotional and physical pain. Always remember, without no pain there is no gain.

I know it sounds easier than what you feel can be done. Hold yourself high one foot after another, you've survived 100% of every bad day, so there's already so much you've overcome.

If you feel no one believes in you, I have this to share with you. I was once just like you. Nothing can stop what you want to do. If you feel like no one else is there to help you along the way. Take a deep breath and remember and let my words help guide you back to your sunny days.

The Awakening Light

As your spiritual awakening steps into the light
with the solar eclipse.
There's a few things you need to do to achieve
Devine's truest gift.
First, you need to let go of what doesn't serve
your inner peace.
The truest of gifts is what lies underneath.
You've been sent a message to stop reflecting in
such a negative light.
All that will be accomplished is karmic energy
that's only full of spite.
You keep asking yourself when will I figure this
life out and finally get things right?
It's not that you're doing anyone wrong with any
ill intent.
It's that you have to go deep within to see what
you are being divinely sent.
Where you pause, reflect and meditate, only then
do you understand.
Deep within you is where you have found the
cards dealt to have the upper hand.
It's to become peaceful towards yourself, full of
pure self-love.
That's when you'll see you have finally heard
the message sent from up above.

It is full of repetitive numbers and spiritual
things.
From animals and nature as far as the eyes can
see.
Now you finally see everything around you with
a positive light.
Now that you're devinely guided, you now
believe everything will be alright.
Now that only positive light shines outward
bound.
All the positive energy will be reflected and
come around.
To everything you want deep within the devines
truest gift.
Always remember these words so you never feel
anything is being missed.
Now you have the knowledge of the lessons that
need to be learned.
Now devinely guided, just be receptive and
you'll see it's now your soul's biggest
fulfillment's turn.

The True Feeling Of Home

As I sit here and write this poem, now I know the true meaning of the feeling of home. It's not inside of anyone else. You just have to look deep into introspection of yourself. All these years it seemed so very far away. Now you've tapped into yourself spiritually and you know it's here to stay.

When someone comes along to add on to that feeling. It is when you finally know your soul has been healed. Stripped away from worldwide belief. You need someone in your life in order to feel complete. This life is full of challenges but we should never feel like we should have to compete. Once you get unwired from society's view of what we should be trapped in their tiny box. You'll see life's true beauty and all that awaits that's now been unlocked.

Loving Yourself From Underneath

Something I heard that rings quite true. Before, you can feel the intensity when someone means the spoken words" I love you. You have to believe in self-love. The first step is loving yourself too.

That's when your heart and mind will be at inner peace. Showing everyone what truly lies underneath.

What's been trapped inside of someone else's view? You've felt so misguided never truly wanting to be you.

Always doing the next thing just to not be judged and to feel like you fit in. All that's done is to build a prison within.

Deep in your heart, mind, body and soul. Everything feels like it's spinning out of control. You've turned your life into a competition. All the whole time, you haven't stopped to see what you're missing.

Stuck in the endless loop of resentment or failure of the past. Stuck in a negative mindset, that's why everything that comes forth never lasts. Always fearing it's too good to be true.

Only because deep down you know you stopped
being authentically you.
You're so used to chaos, trauma and battle scars.
When someone or something comes along that's
true, you find it too hard.
You mistake peace and tranquillity for boredom.
Your head now feels like overwhelming anxiety.
All the immense feeling of pure intensity of love
you've mistaken for toxicity.
That's why I know you self sabotaged and ran
away. Because you don't think you deserve or
are not worthy of love, thinking it will not stay.
Know you can have everything you want and
need in life just take a deep breath.
When you're truly grounded and have faith,
peace, love and happiness, you'll feel your soul
is finally at rest.

The Burning Soul Of A Twin Flame

I don't believe this is truly the end. I believe this
is only a brief separation, until we see each other
again.
Where we pick back up with a clean slate.
Nothing is written in stone and we're the ones
that chooses our fate.
We also know we can't live in the past. Doing so
will just guarantee the journey of our souls
won't last.
We can bring the tools we've learned that will
make this a guaranteed success. Knowing deep
in our hearts that's what seperates our journey
from among the rest.
We felt a deep connection right from the very
start. One that runs deeper than the deepest
feelings from the heart.
We're twin flames mirroring each others soul.
Through the good and the bad, sometimes it
feels like it's spinning out of control.
We need to keep our faith that we've been sent
to one another to heal and grow. Knowing we
are safe and it's finally okay to let go.

Let go of all our past pain because we were
constantly done wrong in the past. We needed to
have these lessons to appreciate love's true song.
I know what others have put us through
definitely wasn't alright. Becoming more
receptive to one another through growth is not
lost in the chaotic ness of fight or flight.
The more we grow, the more we become aware.
That even in those moments, we found life so
unfair.
What we found together in one another is far
beyond compare.
We know what we have deep in our hearts that
we want to share.
Let go of the overthinking of doom that may
await. It's the negative thought patterns that kills
our chances before we've past through loves
gate.
When we think more positively, we'll see what
we have is destined to be true. It also runs
deeper than the words I love you.
We know we can make it together as we already
felt it deep within. Regardless of what others
have to say, we know we can make it to thee
end.
All that really matters is what we both feel and
think. Letting any outside sources in will only
make our ship sink.

To Be Healed Deep Within

Everyone must heal their past trauma if you want a fresh start. Not doing so will just lead to endless cycles of broken hearts. Sit with the experience even if you must feel a little pain. You most likely will thank me one day as you'll learn the lesson to not keep doing this again.

Being with someone too quickly just leads to a quick fix that generally doesn't last. Just as quickly as they came in, they're gone like that, just like the past.

We tend to move on and bury it in our subconscious mind. Thinking it buried for good and will be very hard to find. Unfortunately, that's not the case. You'll see them pop up as later triggers, so please don't act in haste.

Go back as far as the start of your time. Slowly living through all the pain in rewind. It is the only way I found to free the subconscious mind.

You'll slowly see everything that was buried deep. Don't worry, as soon as you're healed you'll be getting much better sleep.

Sitting with the pain. Yes, it is emotional, but the more time passes I feel grateful. Slowly feeling the old weight that's been holding me back, now everything feels more peaceful.

Remove the layers one at a time, you'll see a difference too. Stepping in to fresher light, you'll feel like a happier, more peaceful you.

The other things you'll start to see are negative patterns right from the start. No more passing red flags for green, which will later on save you from a broken heart.

Since all the past trauma is done and gone. Even when the slightest bump tries to steer you wrong. You'll see what I now see that's been there all along.

Now we see right before our very eyes. When anything tries to take us by surprise.

Sit with it for a little while so it can stay in the past. Whether in growth and reconciliation or something new on the horizon this time, you know it will last. So free your subconscious mind and let your conscious mind run free. Feeling alive,free and blissful, there's no better place to be.

Once you've reached this new level of growth, you'll see all along what's been forgotten the most. The true sense of you, the true sense of self. Stemming from self-love your true value is unlike anything else.

You'll feel amazing to see and feel who loves you for truly being you. Of course, you are the most important person to yourself. Time to get unstuck and take yourself off the shelf.

Living every moment, like every day, is a dream come true. You'll see the endless possibilities. Just have faith and be positive, it's as simple as that.

Mirror To My Soul

The day I met you, when I didn't understand yet, I wasn't fully healed. You came into my life and made me feel this time it's for real .
The mirror to my soul. That's why I know we were both easily triggered. We didn't yet know we'd have to walk through a blizzard.
Even though we had more amazing memories than bad. We both got triggered and ran only thinking that's what we had.
We had more peace, love and harmony. The intensity rocked our core. Having both our bad triggers, we each took turns running for the door.
We both said things we didn't mean to say. We said things impulsively feeling we had to run away.
We never called each other names in the heat of the moment. Just stuck in fight or flight, that's what we learned was our safety element.
When the smallest little negative thing crosses our path. Our subconscious mind was stuck in a negative loop. We didn't have the knowledge we do now to figure out the math.
All along, this was a cause of unhealed pain. Not doing the proper healing on both our parts, we had nothing to gain.

Through the time of separation and reconciliation. The word of this needs to spread wide and far right across the nation.

What we have is much more than soulmate energy. Why do we feel each other deep inside to escape past injury?

For everything that's been done wrong to our hearts. We felt an instant chemistry reaction right from the start.

That's also why we can never hide what's wrong. We've both felt it at times, sometimes even without words or songs.

We've empowered each other. We are worthy of love. Know that you and I have been guided together from above.

We've definitely learnt the lessons we were sent. You and me forever. That's what Devine's timing meant. Both together or in separation, deep in thought. We were only meant to be together forever once we learnt what was being taught. I know next time will be forever long. We are now hearing the heartbeat of each others drum. The last of my poem to you goes like this. I miss your touch, I miss your kiss, until you I never knew it was possible to miss everything about someone like this. I truly hope we can be together again. I know we have what it takes to make it to thee end. I love you more than life itself. That's one of many reasons that separates you from everyone else. I love you for exactly who you are. Throughout the entire galaxy, you are my star. The only one who's ever given the feeling of being safe. I know deep down this is our destined fate. We're meant to be together forever. Until we get called, it our time for heavenly gates.